David Gascoyne

Letter To An Adopted Godfather

Edited and introduced by
Roger Scott

etruscan books

First published by etruscan books

Letter to an Adopted Godfather
Letter © Estate of David Gascoyne 2012
Introduction & notes © Roger Scott 2012
Drawing © The estate of Jessica Dismorr, pen and wash drawing, 1930s, exhibited
Mayor Gallery, London 1965 (private collection)

This edition world copyright © etruscan books 2012

COPYRIGHT
No part of this publication may be reproduced
without the prior permission of etruscan books

ISBN   1-901-538-82-6
          978-1-901-538-82-3

etruscan books
Elm House, Stowe Lane,
Exbourne, West Devon
EX20 3RY

www.e-truscan.co.uk
atetruscan@aol.com

Typography: Robert Moore
Printing: Aldgate Press, London

This publication was in part made possible
by a grant from the Arts Council, England

To the memory of Judy Gascoyne February 1 1922 - June 14 2010

THE BOOSTER   MENSUEL

A monthly in French and English

EXECUTIVE and EDITORIAL OFFICES
18, Villa Seurat
Paris (14ᵉ)

EDITORIAL BOARD
Alfred Perlès
Lawrence Durrell
Henry Miller

ASSOCIATE EDITORS
William Saroyan
Anaïs Nin
Hilaire Hiler
Patrick Evans

PUBLICITY
David Edgar

SUBSCRIPTION RATES : France and French Colonies, 1 year 50 fr., 2 years 85 fr. - Great Britain, 1 year 12 shillings, 2 years 1 guinea. - United States and Canada, 1 year 3 dollars, 2 years 5 dollars.

Editorial	5
Announcements	7
Letter for the Gostersools, by Hans Reichel	9
Death, by Gerald Durrell	11
Les Poissons, par Raymond Queneau	12
Limbs Ancient and Modern, by Alfred Perlès	18
How They Buried Petrella, by Patrick Evans	23
A Boost for *Black Spring*, by Anaïs Nin	27
Epilogue to *Black Spring*, by Henry Miller	28
Une Fable, par Oswell Blakeston	32
Blind Man's Buff, by David Gascoyne	34
La Fille de Mᵐᵉ Fechner, par Milada Souckova	37
How to Lead the Podiatric Life, by Henry Miller	39
Poem, Story, Novel, by William Saroyan	41
Notes on New Contributors	49
Poem, by Richard Blake Brown	50

THE BOOSTER is now on sale in the following Paris bookshops

Down-town :   Brentano's, 37, avenue de l'Opéra.
W. H. Smith and Son, 248, rue de Rivoli.
Castiglione Bookstore, rue Castiglione.
Calignani's, 224 rue de Rivoli.

Latin Quarter :   Sylvia Beach, 12, rue de l'Odéon.
José Corti, 11, rue de Médicis.

Montparnasse :   Art et Littérature, 120, boulevard du Montparnasse.
Louis Tschann, 84, boulevard du Montparnasse.

NOVEMBER 1937. - Directeur et Rédacteur en Chef : Alfr. Perlès.
3ᵉ ANNÉE. — N° 9.

INTRODUCTION: David Gascoyne and Henry Miller

Henry Miller takes his place among the literary figures who influenced David Gascoyne to a marked extent, in company with Rimbaud, Pascal, Marx and Freud, Breton, Pierre Jean Jouve and his wife Blanche, and Benjamin Fondane.[1] Like many Americans Miller first made the journey to Paris in the 1920s, and he would live there throughout the next decade. David Gascoyne's first visit to Paris was in 1933.

> *When Cyril Connolly, Henry Miller and Lawrence Durrell were first published in Paris by the Obelisk Press in the mid-1930s, Connolly told Miller that I was a young English Surrealist. Miller sent me a proof copy of* 'Open Letter to Surrealists Everywhere'.[2]

Gascoyne's article 'Henry Miller', a review of *Tropic of Cancer* and *Black Spring*, appeared in *Comment* No. 39 on 19th September 1936. He is fulsome in his praise, but his warm, enthusiastic - if slightly awed - response is tempered by a clear awareness of the need to provide a balanced view of the work and the writer. Referring to Céline's *Voyage an bout de la nuit*, Gascoyne finds in Miller's novels 'the same unbounded pessimism, the same catastrophic vision of a world stifling in disease and filth.' He goes on: 'He has not, however, the same acid and relentless bitterness as Céline, and is not in the least inhuman. I believe Miller's experience is a wider one. It is more generous, more varied, and more intensely lyrical. His lyricism is perhaps his most remarkable characteristic.' However, the twenty-year-old critic finds that both books under review could be accused of formlessness, 'a part of their very nature [...] excused by the intense sincerity of the cry that goes up from them.' Gascoyne identifies Miller's chief weakness: 'his complete indifference to politics, to anything resembling an objective view of society. He realizes that society is falling to pieces, he refuses to believe that there is any hope at all for the future.' As for Miller's importance in the mid-thirties, '[his] writing makes ninety-nine per cent of contemporary novels seem entirely superfluous.'[3]

1 The entry for 27.II-1.III.40, headed *Influences*, notes: '[...] Miller, no doubt, even though only indirectly.'
2 David Gascoyne: obituary for Lawrence Durrell in *The Independent*, 10 November 1990.
3 The review is reprinted in David Gascoyne, *Selected Prose 1934-1996* (London: Enitharmon Press, 1998), pp. 287-89.

Gascoyne arrived in Paris on 7th August 1937, and by the 17th had been settled for more than a week in his garret at 11 rue de la Bûcherie with his window overlooking Notre Dame. In the late summer he went to see Miller in the artists' community at 18 Villa Seurat. They had been introduced some time before by Walter Lowenfels, the American avant-garde poet. There Gascoyne met Lawrence Durrell, and the three writers remained life-long friends until the deaths of the American in 1980 and of Durrell ten years later. Gascoyne was appointed poetry editor of *The Booster*, edited by Alfred Perlès, Miller and Durrell, and also met Anaïs Nin who offered him typing work; both Durrell and Gascoyne figured in Nin's journals, the former 'more favourably and longer', according to Gascoyne.

Gascoyne was persuaded by Nin to publish *Blind Man's Buff* (Fragments from an Unfinished Notebook) in *The Booster*, 3me année, No. 9 (November 1937), which included Miller's visceral and apocalyptic description of the temper of the times in his 'Epilogue' to *Black Spring*. Six poems by Gascoyne, 'Cavatina', 'Venus Androgyne', 'Lowland', 'The Hero', 'Signs', 'The Fault', appeared in *Delta*, successor to *The Booster*, (April 1938), and then his translation, 'The most beautiful most naked and most tragic splendours', from the French of Pierre Jean Jouve in *Delta*, 3me année, No. 1 (Easter 1939).

In January 1939, Gascoyne attended a huge *Front Populaire* Meeting in Paris, then met Miller in Montmartre.

*   *   *

In *Tropic of Cancer* Miller recalls 'those miserable days' when he first arrived in Paris, 'a bewildered, poverty-stricken individual who haunted the streets like a ghost at a banquet' [...] 'the feeling of suffocation'; [...] 'No appointments, no invitations for dinner, no program, no dough.' [...] Each morning the dreary walk to the American Express, and each morning the inevitable answer from the clerk.' [...] 'squeezing my guts to stop the gnawing'. His portrayal chimes with Gascoyne's own depiction of himself in the eleventh paragraph of his 'Letter to H.M.' below, beginning:

> *The point being that during the early days of my last stay in Paris I went through a pretty nasty time. You know the kind of thing: - no food for days on end except a croissant or two, long anxious waitings for the postman but no letters,*

pathetic little notes from the landlady demanding rent slipped under the door every morning, long dream-like walks through strangely hostile-seeming nocturnal streets, an endless gaping sickness in the stomach and a gnawing beneath the breast. This was in August and September, and practically all the people I had known in Paris before seemed to be out of town on holiday [...]'

The typescript from which my transcription below was made is undated. However, it would appear that Gascoyne composed it in 1941 at the latest, or at the end of the thirties (but see footnote 5 on page 8). An Ms 'Notebook, 1941', lists an anthology, 'The Naked Eye', one of his abandoned projects, planned as follows:

1. People and Places; 2. Psychological; 3. Philosophical I; 4. Philosophical II; 5. On Poetry; 7 [sic]. General & Miscellaneous AND Extracts from a Commonplace Book.

On various pages Gascoyne sets out the proposed contents of 'The Naked Eye' in three modified versions I have named A, B, C, each of which includes the letter to Henry Miller which may never have been sent and is here published for the first time:

(A) I Blind Man's Buff; II Texts in Context 1; III The Subjective Thinker; IV Texts in Context 2; V *Letter to an Adopted Godfather*; VI Texts in Context 3; VII Phenomena of Zero OR Miscellaneous Marginalia.

(B) I Blind Man's Buff; II The Chamber of Maiden-Thought; III The Subjective Thinker & Experimental Introspection; IV The Phenomena of Zero; [V]; VI *Letter to an Adopted Godfather*; VII Miscellaneous Marginalia; VIII From a Commonplace Book.

(C) 1. Blind Man's Buff; 2. The Subjective Thinker; 3. The Phenomena of Zero; 4. *Epistle to Hentry Miller*; 5. Marginalia: Memorabilia: Muddle [sic]; 6. Outline of a Poetic [sic]; 7. Pièces de Demonstration.

Roger Scott

November 2011

LETTER TO AN ADOPTED GODFATHER[4]

Dear H. M.,

For how long have I been meaning, and really intending, to write you something like a letter? Years. And all the while, though not continuously, there has been developing at the back of my general lurid recollection of you and your writing the procrastinated determination to write a book that you might be able to consider to be *on your own level*. I have desultorily filled exercise-books labelled *Journal*. I have scribbled in notebooks of assorted sizes; I have accumulated a heap of random scraps and notes amounting to much more than a mere mole-hill, yet all this seemed to me increasingly inescapable proof that I should never write *the book*. I indeed despaired. By the middle of the War[5] I had reached a state of semi-stupefaction in which the hope of ever making ultimate coherence seemed scarcely to be of interest any longer, except during brief weekends of resurrected solitary enthusiasm. All things considered, however, it seems to me now, there may have been much mercy in this relapse into apparent embers of my early creative urge.

There are, however, definite reasons for my wanting temporarily to adopt a Father, and for my choosing you. To begin with, for this kind of writing I need someone to address myself to, someone to whom I can say 'you' every now and again. I want very much to *explain* myself, and am sick of doing so merely to the empty air. I cannot do so to my real father, because he is a reserved sort of man (a bank-clerk, as it happens) who has a strong dislike of any such intrusion on his intimacy, and although he can manage to stomach my being a 'highbrow' writer, I am sure that this kind of writing would temporarily upset him, somehow. So I have to look around for a suitable person.

But why should I pick on *you*, perhaps you are asking, with puzzled amusement, or with indignation?

(I am trying at this moment to picture you in your studio at the Villa Seurat, clad in your green velvet gardening hat and your

---

4   The original is part of the David Gascoyne Special Collection at the Beinecke Rare Book and Manuscript Library, Yale University, Box 5, Folder 63, fo. 5.
5   'By the middle of the War' suggests that Gascoyne made modifications to the original letter after the War, or that it was unwritten in 1941.

disgraceful old dressing-gown, as you were that day when I came round to say goodbye before last leaving Paris, much engrossed in Balzac's *Seraphina*, and with your indescribable eyes twinkling away like tadpoles behind your oddly schoolmasterish spectacles. I say 'indescribable' only out of laziness. Actually they are *knowing*; but to explain what I meant by that would involve an explanation (not to you!) of all the meaning one can attach to Nietzsche's expression: *le gai savoir.*)

I cannot think of any good reason why it should interest or impress you very much to be told that I consider you to be *a great man* and have had this opinion ever since I first met you, so I will mention this fact only just in passing. (Incidentally, I have met disappointingly few other 'great' men, so far as I know. One of these was André Breton; Eluard was another; Picasso, Pierre Jean Jouve; and Benjamin Fondane, a great metaphysical temperament whom you did not, I think, altogether appreciate, when I first introduced him to you, and who still seems strangely unrecognized.) Apart from this fact, I have chosen to address this document to you rather than to anyone else because, after all, you were one of the first people to help me to form a really clear conception of *what I want to be*. I want to be my own self, to the very limit of my identity, and so, of course, I have had to set about discovering this identity of mine. The identity one is born with is only the raw material with which to create, since it is one's 'vocation' to do so, a more profound, *responsible*, identity. And curious though it may seem to you, one of the first things to help me realize inescapably that my chief desire in life was to establish a unique and unmistakable identity, was something which I read of yours in which you described how you first went to Paris and knew that you had to break away from everything that had seemed to be your life until then; to break away like part of a star breaking away to become a new star with an orbit of its own, in order to become wholly and solely your own indestructible, eccentric, vitalizing self.

It seems to me now that one's quest for one's self is a never ending one. What matters, I suppose, is to get started and, once started, to keep on perpetually, to keep perpetually starting again, even though there may not be very much hope of finding a *truly complete man* in the end. If one is always in motion in that sense, one can at any rate claim to exist, which is no common achievement. (As I see it, existence is a strenuous and whole-time occupation).

Since the fundamental characteristic of my personal identity is the continual conflict going on between the two sides of my deeply divided nature, to exist (in the positive sense) entails, for me, following both these sides of my nature to their contradictory extremes. I continually risk being torn in half in an attempt to resolve the contradiction between my life and my thought. To persevere in all these contradictions is often very painful, tedious and bewildering. What keeps me going is above all the fundamental desire in me to live my own life, no matter how strange and unpleasant this life may turn out to be. And this desire represents the best explanation of why I am adopting you for the time being as my Father; because, as I have said, you were one of the first exterior forces to give it a definite stimulus.

I don't want to write a lot of nonsense about your 'teaching' or your 'spiritual position'. I know quite well that you don't care a damn whether other people live their own lives or find their precious individual selves or not, so long as they leave you in peace to live your own life and to be yourself. But I thought I'd like just to tell you something about how, incidentally, you encouraged me in my looking about for a chair of my own to sit down on. I am telling you about it without any regard for your feelings, simply because it happens to be *necessary to me* at the moment to express myself in this way. It is my way of sitting down. (Very well, for the sake of politeness, then, since I was born with a certain rather ridiculous sense of politeness which makes itself evident only on unnecessary occasions: – Will you kindly excuse my sitting down?)

I well remember the first occasion on which I set out to visit you at the Villa Seurat. We had already corresponded a little, and you had sent me a copy of *Black Spring*, a book by which I had been much disturbed. I had lived in Paris before, for short spells at a time, and although I believe I was introduced to you once during my first visit by Walter L.[owenfels], I could barely remember this when I came to live in Paris in 1937 (with nothing to live on). I came over 'to see the Exhibition' with some friends, and then, as I had previously decided to do, when they returned to England, I stayed on in Paris alone.

Fortunately, one of my friends had left me a few pounds to go on with.

On the very first night after finding myself completely alone in Paris with hardly any cash and no plans for the future except a grim determination to go on being there even at the cost of starvation, I got picked up as I was going back to my attic by a couple of whores,[6] who seemed to think I was a wealthy, soft-hearted, innocent English schoolboy-tourist (I may even have looked like one). I went off with them to a dirty little hotel, not because I wanted to fuck them – as you can well imagine from what you already know of me: I have not got a furious appetite for fucking, certainly not with two whores at once, and I'm not really interested in quite that way in the female sex, anyway – but because I had some crazy, pseudo-Dostoievskian idea that the occasion might afford me with an opportunity to explore certain 'lower depths'. I suppose it was, in fact, quite an interesting occasion, really: I told the whores I wanted simply to have a friendly chat, and they thereupon behaved in a typically curious way: pulled my hair, had mild hysterics, squatted on the bidet, wept on my shoulder, told me sentimentally decorated and therefore doubly horrible life-stories, and soon. We all drank a lot of bad wine, and finally we parted on quite friendly terms and went our ways, I with a lucky charm in my pocket made of a lock of one of the girls' hair tied through a sou, and the whores with all my money except the fifty francs with which I was supposed to be paying the first week's rent of my attic.

All this is rather too discursive and beside the point. The point being that during the early days of my last stay in Paris I went through a pretty nasty time. You know the kind of thing: – no food for days on end except a croissant or two, long anxious waitings for the postman but no letters, pathetic little notes from the landlady demanding rent slipped under the door every morning, long dream-like walks through strangely hostile-seeming nocturnal streets, an endless gaping sickness in the stomach and a gnawing beneath the breast. This was in August and September, and practically all the people I had known in Paris

---

6   Gascoyne sent a description of this same incident to Antonia White in a letter headed 'Paris, August 1937'. Here he describes the women as 'a pair of Communist prostitutes'. As they parted, Gascoyne writes, they said 'Il faut être vache, chéri!', and he adds, 'and after all they have to be. We gave one another the clenched fist salute, and parted friends.'

before seemed to be out of town on holiday. The few people I knew whom I did manage to run into were mostly Frenchmen whom I did not feel I could possibly ask to 'lend' me money. It was on one of these sort of days that I remembered that I'd got your address in my pocket, and that I wanted to meet you anyway, and that if one was to believe what you wrote, you were not likely to be very surprised or annoyed to be asked for an occasional meal. So in the evening I got up in rather a weak condition from my stuffy couch and set out on that long walk, which I know so well by now, from the Seine to the Parc Montsouris: all along the rue St. Jacques and the rue du Faubourg St. Jacques, a purgatorial route appropriately lined with butcher's shops, hospitals, clinics, and convents. It was dark by the time I got to the Villa Seurat; I rang your bell, but it seemed to be out of order; I stumbled into the front hall, but couldn't find the *minuterie*; and ultimately reached your door, though in the darkness I couldn't read the portentous inscription on it until I struck a match. There was no answer to my knocking. Perhaps you were in bed with someone: if so, the noise I made coming up the stairs would certainly have made you pause to gasp exacerbatedly while waiting for me to decamp. Anyway, in the end I traipsed away again, back to my room, by way of redly-glaring Montparnasse. It was one of those quiet, familiar evenings when I used to feel lost at the bottom of a tiny black hole in the floor of the universe.

I went back to my room. And it occurs to me now that *it was always the same room* to which I returned. I mean that the part of my disordered but outwardly placid existence to which I used to attach the highest degree of reality was the part which I lived invisibly and in utter solitude. Between the four walls of a room; not in the *hallucinating open street*, which I saw, when I walked through it, in the most vividly disturbing colour and detail, but also as though from the other side of a plate of unbreakable glass. The glass would break and vanish only when I found myself at last alone again in a room, and it was always the same room. It did not matter whether the windows looked out over a gothic cathedral or over a nondescript suburban garden, or whether it was a reproduction of a Dürer etching that I could see pinned to the wall at the foot of my bed or a poster-colour panel designed by one of the most gifted of my homosexual friends. Sometimes there seemed to be a hideous pinewood wardrobe facing the corner where I lay and might have beheld my lanky and angular nakedness reflected in the fly-blown, tarnished mirror on the wardrobe door, or again, there may have been thick, dark plush curtains and a tattered screen in the other corner of the room, and on the opposite wall the mysterious enlarged shadow of the whirling cigarette-smoke I lay breathing from my mouth. Now and then there would come a change in the quality of the light: sometimes it was the deadly light of a wet, grey early morning, the relentless light reflected on a guillotine's poised blade; but most often it seemed to be just past midnight, and either the room would be filled with the thin, tepid glare of a single shadeless bulb hung high up close to the ceiling, or else I would be with half-closed eyes within the more comforting circular radiance of a small red-shaded bedside-lamp. But regardless of these superficial appearances, it was always undoubtedly *the same room* in which I lay, or sat reclining on my elbow, attempting to read some book I was probably sick of the sight of, smoking chains of cigarettes, occasionally scribbling a few notes in an exercise-book.

The familiar, senseless, centreless pain in my left side is throbbing away like a gentle but exhausting dynamo. It may be that suddenly I am seized with a wild desire to break bodily asunder, and to go rushing with all the force of an emotional explosion out through the windows, in hurtled fragments of flesh and bone to go rushing out into the distant world upon the wings of the wind of 4 a.m. But nothing happens. I remain quite motionless, and dark, undefined and flabby shapes begin to press down upon my eyelids. Presently I get up to go and make some tea, or drop off into a sleep in which I am disturbed by dreaming that my heart is beating at ten times its normal speed .....

This kind of thing has been going on almost nightly for years now, and very often during long-drawn-out daytimes as well, in one place or another; but wherever it may be situated, it is always the same room. No unexpected visitor has ever come to knock upon the door of this lethal chamber, and I do not think that there is much chance that anyone ever will.

The surburban bedrooms, the attics and hotel rooms in which I have stayed and lived, manufacturing in them the rare but stifling atmosphere of my solitudes, have all been the same to the extent that they have all been an image of that securely locked isolation-cell[7] in which the inadaptable self of the schizophrene is transported ever further and more irrevocably away from the sense of reality of his so-called normal self outside. The prisoned self is well aware of the catastrophe threatened by this ever-widening distance, but no matter how much he may rave and beat against the bars, it is unlikely that he will ever be able to make himself heard or to call a halt to the stealthy withdrawal of the real world from which he is exiled by forces he cannot control.

I am in the same room at the moment, composing this letter.

I am trying to grope my way through all the unavoidable obscurities towards the central point of what I am trying to express.

I cannot become resigned. I cannot accept –*what?* I cannot accept *the fact of my own impotence.*

Impotence. That is what it is that burns, day in day out, like a white-hot iron at the core of my identity: my consciousness of impotence. Impotent to couple with the reality of the objective world. Impotent to impose my own reality upon the reality outside. Impotent to overthrow the tyranny of abstract forces such as Reason and Necessity. Impotent either to alter the restricting circumstances of my existence, or to accept them as they are ..... And so many other forms of impotence, by implication, all amounting in the end to this: that I am impotent to *go out of my mind* as in my most secret self I long to do, because I am for ever frustrated by the firmly-rooted integrity of my intelligence. I have tried calmly to find out what are various possible solutions to the problem of how to continue to exist. It seems there are not many ways out, but one has to choose one of them sooner or later, even though involuntarily, even though one may refuse in the name of freedom to be forced to choose at all (in which case, the best thing one can do is abandon one's mental responsibility; avoid being aware of choosing). The only alternatives that I can think of are: Physical suicide. The sleep of resignation, the abandonment of all disturbing mental awareness. One or another form of compromise. Or else: the perpetual strain of non-resignation, non-acceptance of necessity.

---

7   In his journal entry for 1.VIII.37 he had written: 'Never in my life have I felt so isolated, so utterly petrifyingly solitary.'

As far as I can see, your own principal concern is to make yourself comfortable and contented within the womb of the real world; and you achieve this partly by philosophic, Aristotelian resignation to and acceptance of Necessity (for this is what your *living in the present*, your cries of excitement and wonder in face of of the spectacle of existence, amount to); partly by camouflaging reality and disguising it from yourself, that is to say by gilding the bitter pill by means of the imagination.

Personally, I cannot pretend that my first concern has ever been contentment. Even the highest form of contentment that one can achieve on earth seems to me to be much like a kind of narcotic stupor, that I could never bear to live in it for long. I have always had a sense (of *Le Bonheur divin*) a sense which seems almost like a mysterious recollection of the state preceding birth, and that is what I really want, and I can never hope to be satisfied with anything else. And so: drama, strain and anguish without end. An ever-latent Claustrophobia caused by the walls of the world-womb [*phrase missing*] – in order to persevere I must have faith, *ex nihilo*, in spite of everything.

This ounce of faith is one of the rare concessions to the instinctive human demand for comfort that I can at all willingly allow myself to make.

You attribute man's misery to the fact that he allows himself to be the prey of unreal abstractions, do you not? The inexorable abstractions bred by moralists, ethicists, philosophers, critics, lawyers, politicians, etc. We are sucked dry and sterile by ideas as though by vampires. Therefore we must rid ourselves of our exaggerated awe of them, cease to attribute more than a secondary and quite relative importance to their authority, refuse to admit the validity of their unremitting claim to determine human behaviour (without succeeding in doing so, except quite superficially). Then we shall be able to live in and enjoy the only true reality, which is that of most immediate present experience.

But, of course, *vous êtes de votre occident* as R.[8] would say, even in

---

8 A reference to Rimbaud for whom Gascoyne and Miller shared a mutual admiration. Gascoyne is quoting a line from Rimbaud's poem 'L'Impossible' from *Une Saison en enfer*, used by Benjamin Fondane as the epigraph to Chapter XIX of his *Rimbaud le voyou*. Miller's *The Time of the Assassins: A Study of Rimbaud* was published years later in 1956.

holding this point of view. On what do you base your argument against abstractions, if not on one or another of these very abstractions? (Unless once more you base it on a primary concern for comfort.)

Although I unhesitatingly agree with you as to the vital necessity of inoculating oneself once and for all against the hideous poison of abstractions (while also admitting and deploring the fact that the origin of any opinion can be traced back to this very poison), I have never been able to believe that it is quite so easy to do so as you sometimes appear to pretend. The Reason, the prime source of all abstractions, has practically become an additional instinct in civilized man. [*Illegible*] tension, like an explosion, – a clap of thunder, out of which the transcendental grace that was referred to will descend upon one like a tongue of flame .....

I need hardly add that if I seem perhaps to be making an unusual amount of fuss and protest and lamentation, – if my gesture of refusal to accept *things as they are* seems almost absurdly in earnest, – this is not, of course, so much because I am striving to be consistent with my thought as because my thought is indirectly an expression of my character, heredity, education, neurotic constitution etc; similarly, the fundamental sanity and serenity, the spontaneous joy of living, which have always impressed me so deeply in your own outlook, do not in any sense represent the results of your *Weltanschauung*: rather are they the factors which more than anything else have determined its development. Your despair most closely resembles a triumphant and exalted affirmation of deep-rooted life; while my own is a cheerless, anguished, furiously reiterated refusal to accept the conditions not only of man's life in general but also of my own life in particular, and this difference is really to be explained not as a philosophical one, but rather as one between two temperaments far too dissimilar by nature ever to to able to reach a mutually satisfying polemical agreement, except perhaps by means of inspired grace .....

[*Typescript ends here*]